the TECHNOLOGY beHIND

MACHINES OF SPEED AND FLIGHT

Nicolas Brasch

- ➲ How Do Hot-Air Balloons Work?
- ➲ What Is a Four-Stroke Engine?
- ➲ Can Spy Planes Fly Without Being Detected?

A+

This edition first published in 2011 in the United States of America by Smart Apple Media.
All rights reserved. No part of this book may be reproduced in any form or by any means without
written permission from the publisher.

Smart Apple Media
P.O. Box 3263
Mankato, MN, 56002

First published in 2010 by
MACMILLAN EDUCATION AUSTRALIA PTY LTD
15–19 Claremont St, South Yarra, Australia 3141

Visit our web site at www.macmillan.com.au or go directly to www.macmillanlibrary.com.au

Associated companies and representatives throughout the world.

Copyright © Nicolas Brasch

Library of Congress Cataloging-in-Publication Data

Brasch, Nicolas.
    Machines of speed and flight / Nicolas Brasch.
        p. cm. — (The technology behind)
    Includes index.
    ISBN 978-1-59920-568-7 (library bound)
    1. Motor vehicles—Juvenile literature. 2. Airplanes—Juvenile literature.
    3. Space vehicles—Juvenile literature. I. Title.
    TL147.B73 2011
629.04'6—dc22

                                                    2009054434

Publisher: Carmel Heron
Managing Editor: Vanessa Lanaway
Editor: Georgina Garner
Proofreader: Erin Richards
Designer: Stella Vassiliou
Page layout: Stella Vassiliou and Raul Diche
Photo researcher: Wendy Duncan (management: Debbie Gallagher)
Illustrators: Alan Laver, pp. 7, 8, 9, 10, 11, 13, 16, 17, 18, 21, 22 (top), 24, 25, 26, 27, 28, 29, 30, 31;
    Richard Morden, p. 22 (bottom); Karen Young, p. 1 and Try This! logo.
Production Controller: Vanessa Johnson

Manufactured in China by Macmillan Production (Asia) Ltd.
Kwun Tong, Kowloon, Hong Kong
Supplier Code: CP March 2010

Acknowledgements

The author and the publisher are grateful to the following for permission to reproduce copyright material:

Front cover photographs:
Car © Shutterstock/Dawid Konopka; Plane © David Liu/iStockphoto; Rocket, NASA/courtesy of
nasaimages.org.

© Aero Graphics, Inc./Corbis, **23**; © Bob Daemmrich/Corbis, **12** (top); © Laurent Hamels/PhotoAlto/
Corbis, **20**; © Richard Olivier/Corbis, **14**; © Transtock/Corbis, **19**; © Dreamstime/Noahgolan, **12** (bottom
left); © Tom Brown/iStockphoto, **12** (bottom right); © Graham Heywood/iStockphoto, **6** (right); © David
Liu/iStockphoto, **5** (bottom); © Shaun Lowe/iStockphoto, **5** (top); © Cliff Parnell/iStockphoto, **17**; © Liu
Jin/AFP/Getty Images, **8**; NASA/courtesy of nasaimages.org, **26**, **30**; photolibrary/North Wind Photos, **6**
(left); © Shutterstock, **24** (left); © Shutterstock/Eduard Härkönen, **15** (both).

While every care has been taken to trace and acknowledge copyright, the publisher tenders their
apologies for any accidental infringement where copyright has proved untraceable. Where the attempt
has been unsuccessful, the publisher welcomes information that would redress the situation.

The publisher would like to thank Heidi Ruhnau, Head of Science at Oxley College, for her assistance in
reviewing manuscripts.

Please note
At the time of printing, the Internet addresses appearing in this book were correct. Owing to the dynamic
nature of the Internet, however, we cannot guarantee that all these addresses will remain correct.

▶ Contents

Look out for these features throughout the book:

Word Watch

"Word Watch" explains the meanings of words shown in **bold**

Web Watch ▼

"Web Watch" provides web site suggestions for further research

What Is Technology?

The First Tools

One of the first examples of technology, where humans used their knowledge of the world to their advantage, was when humans began shaping and carving stone and metals into tools such as axes and chisels.

▲ People use technology every day, such as when they turn on computers. Technology is science put into action to help humans and solve problems.

Technology is the use of **science** for practical purposes, such as building bridges, inventing machines, and improving materials. Humans have been using technology since they built the first shelters and lit the first fires.

Technology in People's Lives

Technology is behind many things in people's everyday lives, from lightbulbs to can openers. It has shaped the sports shoes people wear and helped them run faster. Cars, trains, airplanes, and space shuttles are all products of technology. Engineers use technology to design and construct materials and structures such as bridges, roads, and buildings. Technology can be seen in amazing built structures all around humans.

Technology is responsible for how people communicate with each other. Information technology uses scientific knowledge to determine ways to spread information widely and quickly. Recently, this has involved the creation of the Internet, and e-mail and file-sharing technologies. In the future, technology may become even more a part of people's lives, with the development of robots and artificial intelligence for use in business, in the home, and in science.

Word Watch

science knowledge that humans have gathered about the physical and natural world and how it works

The Technology Behind Machines of Speed and Flight

Since the wheel was invented, there has been a remarkable series of inventions and discoveries that have helped humans sail the seas, travel the land, fly the skies, and even enter space.

Going Faster and Higher

Machines of speed and flight have changed the world. The invention of the steam-powered train in the late 1700s made it possible for people to travel long distances and transport goods from one place to another. Today, we can take a flight anywhere, and every day billions of people drive cars powered by four-stroke engines.

Technologies of speed and flight are still developing. Car safety is being improved by work with crash-test dummies, pilots use autopilot technology to help fly their planes, and the reusable space shuttle has taken over from disposable rockets. Other, newer technologies are still improving. Maglev trains are used in some cities of the world, and solar car technology is being developed. Humans now have the ability to travel anywhere on Earth—as well as beyond it—but they are still trying to move farther, faster, and higher.

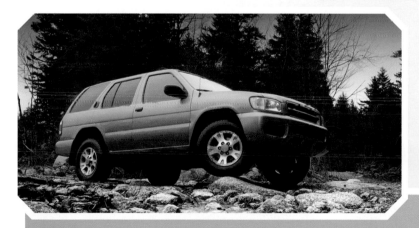

◀ Technology has given us cars that can travel off-road.

▼ Airplane technology means that people can travel all around the world.

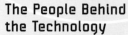

The People Behind the Technology

Many people with different jobs are behind the technology of machines of speed and flight.

Aeronautical Engineer Designing and **overseeing** the construction of planes and other flying machines

Rocket Scientist Designing and overseeing the construction of space rockets

Automotive Designer Designing the appearance and safety features of motor vehicles

Test Pilot Flying newly designed planes to check that they do the job they were designed to do

Word **W**atch

overseeing supervising or watching over

Why Was the Steam Engine Such an Important Invention?

The first steam engine was invented in the 1660s. This technology eventually changed the world. From 1804 forward, steam-powered trains were able to travel farther and faster than any land transportation that had existed before them.

Trains Before Steam

The first steam-powered **locomotives** were not the first trains. The first trains were built by mining companies. They used wooden and later iron tracks along which carriages ran. The tracks started on an **incline** and ran downhill to the end of the line. A driver controlled the speed by applying the brake when needed, and horses were used to pull the carriages back to the top of the incline. They were used on land, under the ground, and from the mine to the nearest river or seaport.

Inventing the Steam Engine

James Watt is considered the "father of the steam engine" although he did not invent it. In the 1770s, he improved on the works of other inventors such as Denis Papin, Thomas Savery, and Thomas Newcomen.

▲ The invention of the steam engine meant people and goods could be transported long distance as well as to and from places that had once been isolated.

◄ The first trains transported coal, minerals, equipment, and people from one area of a mine to another.

How a Steam-Powered Train Works

Steam engine technology was applied to trains in the late 1700s and early 1800s.

Combustion Engines

A steam engine is a type of engine known as an external **combustion** engine. This is because the burning process (the conversion of heat to **motion**) takes place outside the engine. Car engines are internal combustion engines, because the conversion process takes place inside the engine.

3. The chimney also releases steam from the cylinder. The release of this steam is what creates the "choo-choo" noise of a steam train.

2. The heat from the coal boils the water in the boiler. This creates steam. Pipes in the boiler transport the steam down into the cylinder.

1. When coal is burned, it releases energy in the form of heat. In the firebox, coal is burned at a temperature of 2,550°F (1,400°C). The smoke that results from this process escapes through the chimney.

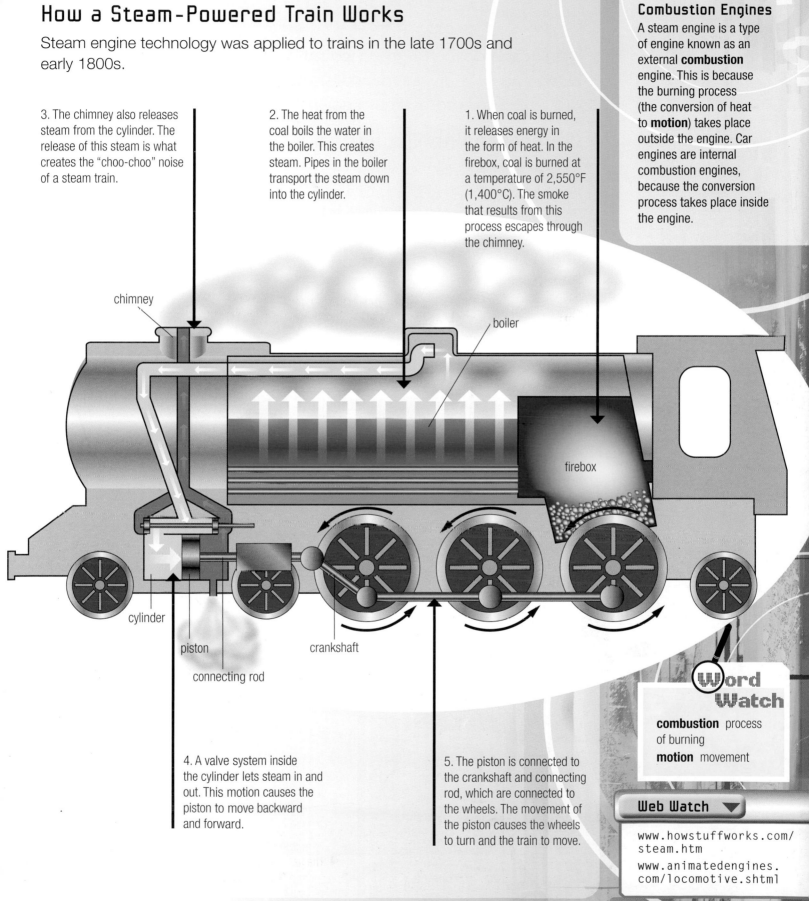

chimney

boiler

firebox

cylinder

piston

connecting rod

crankshaft

4. A valve system inside the cylinder lets steam in and out. This motion causes the piston to move backward and forward.

5. The piston is connected to the crankshaft and connecting rod, which are connected to the wheels. The movement of the piston causes the wheels to turn and the train to move.

Word Watch

combustion process of burning

motion movement

Web Watch ▼

www.howstuffworks.com/steam.htm

www.animatedengines.com/locomotive.shtml

How Do Trains Levitate?

Maglev stands for magnetic **levitation**. Maglev trains do not run along tracks. They use magnetism to hover above them. Because of this, they are sometimes known as hover trains.

Understanding Magnetism

Magnetism is a **force** that draws objects toward each other or pushes them away from each other. This force works because of the presence of a metal that contains magnetic qualities. Some metals with magnetic qualities are iron, cobalt, and nickel.

▶ All magnets have a north pole and a south pole. Unlike poles attract and like poles **repel**. In other words, the north pole of one magnet and the south pole of another magnet will attract each other, but two north poles or two south poles will repel each other.

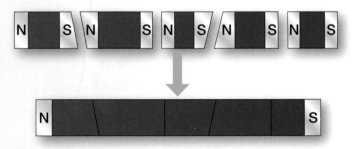

▲ A maglev train hovers over its track in Shanghai, in eastern China.

How a Maglev Train Works

Most maglev trains use one of two types of technology: electromagnetic suspension or electrodynamic suspension.

Electromagnetic Suspension

Electromagnetic suspension (EMS) uses magnetic attraction as its basis. The bottom of the train wraps around the rail, also called a guideway. **Electromagnets** in the undercarriage of the train pull the train toward the steel track, but an electrical current tightly controls the level of attraction and makes sure there is always a distance of 0.3 to 0.4 inch (8–10 mm) between the train and track. An electric motor **propels** the train forward.

Electrodynamic Suspension

Electrodynamic suspension (EDS) uses repulsive force as the basis of its technology. Electromagnets are positioned along the undercarriage and sides of the train, as well as along the guideway. The repulsive force of the electromagnets keeps the train about 4 inches (10 cm) above the track—far higher than the EMS system. Another major difference is that the electromagnets also provide the propulsion that creates forward and backward movement.

First Maglev Trains

The first maglev train trials took place in Germany in 1979, and the first maglev system for passengers was built at Birmingham Airport in England in 1984. There are currently maglev train systems operating in Japan, China, and South Korea.

Word Watch

electromagnets magnets that are powered by an electrical current

propels pushes forward

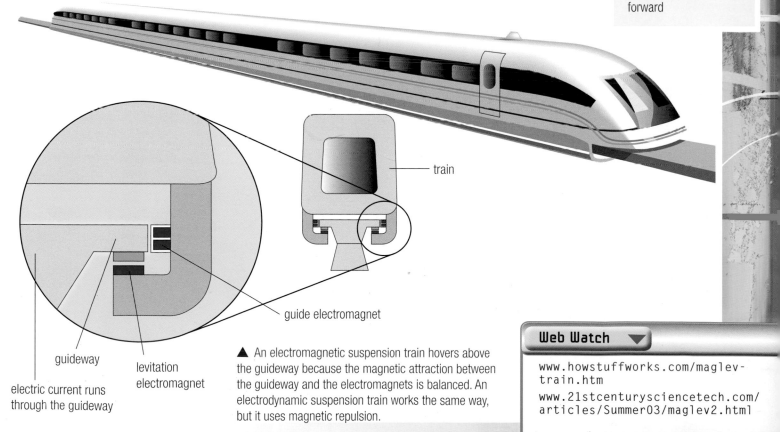

train

guide electromagnet

guideway

levitation electromagnet

electric current runs through the guideway

▲ An electromagnetic suspension train hovers above the guideway because the magnetic attraction between the guideway and the electromagnets is balanced. An electrodynamic suspension train works the same way, but it uses magnetic repulsion.

Web Watch ▼

www.howstuffworks.com/maglev-train.htm

www.21stcenturysciencetech.com/articles/Summer03/maglev2.html

What Is a Four-Stroke Engine?

Most cars use a four-stroke **combustion** engine. A combustion engine works by converting heat into **motion**. The four strokes are the four stages of the cycle.

Combustion Engines

There are two types of combustion engines: internal and external. A car engine is an internal combustion engine, because the conversion process takes place inside the engine. An example of an external combustion engine is a steam engine (see pages 6–7).

Parts of an Engine

All the parts of a car engine depend on each other and play a role in the combustion that powers the car.

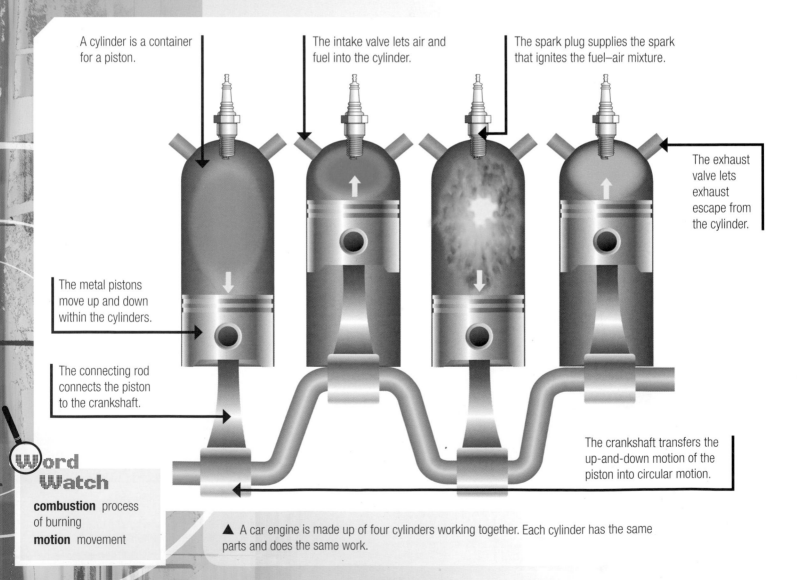

A cylinder is a container for a piston.

The intake valve lets air and fuel into the cylinder.

The spark plug supplies the spark that ignites the fuel–air mixture.

The exhaust valve lets exhaust escape from the cylinder.

The metal pistons move up and down within the cylinders.

The connecting rod connects the piston to the crankshaft.

The crankshaft transfers the up-and-down motion of the piston into circular motion.

▲ A car engine is made up of four cylinders working together. Each cylinder has the same parts and does the same work.

The Four-Stroke Cycle

A four-stroke engine operates on a four-stroke cycle.

1 »» Intake

The piston moves down, allowing fuel and air to enter the cylinder through the open intake valve.

intake valve

fuel–air mixture

piston

2 »» Compression

The piston moves upward, **compressing** the fuel and air, and the intake valve closes. The compression of the fuel and air makes it highly explosive.

compressed fuel and air

piston

3 »» Power (Combustion)

As the piston reaches the top, the spark plug ignites the fuel–air mixture, causing it to explode and creating gases that drive the piston back down the cylinder. The motion of the piston turns the crankshaft, which is connected to the car's gearbox. This process converts energy in the form of heat into **mechanical** energy.

spark plug

explosion

piston

crankshaft

4 »» Exhaust

When the piston reaches the bottom of the cylinder, the exhaust valve opens. The turning of the crankshaft forces the piston up, pushing waste gases (exhaust fumes) through the open exhaust valve. When the cylinder is empty, the process starts all over again.

exhaust valve

exhaust fumes

Many Cylinders Working Together

Most cars have four cylinders. The cylinders do the same job but they are always at different stages of the four-stroke cycle. At any one time, each of the four cylinders is at one of the four strokes, so the power is produced smoothly and continuously.

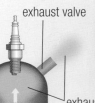

Word Watch

compressing pressing things together into a smaller space

mechanical related to machines, machinery, and physical work

Web Watch ▼

www.animatedengines.com/otto.shtml

What Are the Advantages of Solar Cars?

Solar cars do not run on gasoline. They run on power from the sun. Until now, solar cars have been built to demonstrate solar energy technology, rather than for everyday use. However, as oil becomes scarce and more expensive, solar cars could be the solution!

▲ Two solar cars compete in a race across the United States and Canada.

Solar Power

Solar cars work by capturing the sun's energy and turning it into electricity. Energy comes from the sun as different types of electromagnetic **radiation**. The types of radiation that are used to produce electricity are heat waves and light rays.

Energy in the form of heat is called thermal energy. Thermal energy is captured and converted into electricity, using solar panels or mirrors.

Solar cars do not run on electricity converted from thermal energy. They operate on electricity converted from light captured in solar cells. When **particles** of light enter a solar cell, they create activity among the **electrons** within the cell. It is this activity that generates electricity.

◄ Light rays are captured by solar cells known as photovoltaic cells. A solar panel is made up of a number of photovoltaic cells.

◄ A common item that uses photovoltaic cells is a solar calculator.

How a Solar Car Works

A solar car makes electricity while the sun is shining and stores the electricity in a battery. By storing electricity, the car can be driven on days with low sunlight.

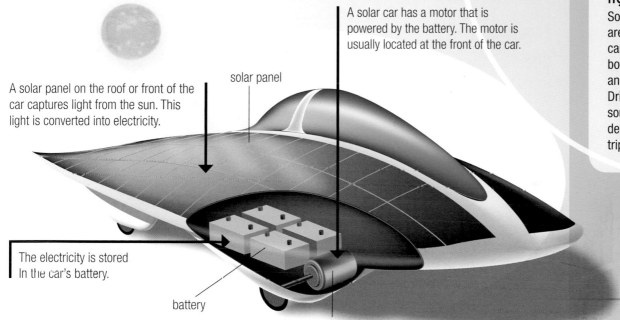

A solar panel on the roof or front of the car captures light from the sun. This light is converted into electricity.

A solar car has a motor that is powered by the battery. The motor is usually located at the front of the car.

solar panel

The electricity is stored In the car's battery.

battery

motor

Hybrid Cars

Some car manufacturers are now producing hybrid cars. Hybrid cars contain both an electric motor and a gasoline engine. Drivers can choose which source of energy to use, depending on the type of trip they have to make.

Advantages and Disadvantages

Generating electricity from the sun is only one way to create electricity to power cars. There are both advantages and disadvantages to electric-powered cars compared to gas-driven cars.

Advantages

✓ Unlike gasoline-driven cars, electric-powered cars do not produce greenhouse gases. This makes them better for the environment.

✓ Electric cars are quieter than gasoline-driven cars, so there is less noise pollution.

✓ Electrical power can be produced from resources that will never run out, such as sunlight, wind, and water.

✓ Electric cars have fewer parts so are cheaper to maintain.

Disadvantages

✗ Electric cars can only travel about 90 miles (150 km) before their batteries need recharging. Gasoline-driven cars can travel more than 370 miles (600 km) before they need to be refilled.

✗ Gasoline is a relatively cheap source of fuel to produce.

✗ Gasoline is easy to transport and store.

Web Watch ▼

poweredbysolarpanels.com/
how-do-the-solar-powered-
cars-work

How Does a Crash-Test Dummy Work?

A crash-test dummy is a **device** shaped like a human that is used to determine what happens to a human body in a car crash. A dummy is made from plastic, metal, and rubber and contains instruments that measure movement and **force**.

Instruments

There are two main types of instruments inside crash-test dummies: accelerometers and sensors. These instruments are connected to computers that record the **data** that is collected.

Accelerometers

Accelerometers measure the **acceleration** of various parts of a person's body in a crash. They measure the speed of movement in all directions. For example, a person's head can move forward, backward, and to the side during a crash. Accelerometers contain tiny magnets that generate electricity when they move. Bursts of electricity indicate the speed at which a body part is moving.

Sensors

Sensors measure the force that various body parts are hit with during a crash. For example, some sensors specifically measure how much the chest is pushed in during a crash. Sensors contain tiny crystals that stretch and squeeze.

Small, Medium, and Large Dummies

Crash test dummies come in various sizes, so that the impact of a crash can be measured on all types of people. The dummy that is used as the driver in most test crashes is 5 feet 10 inches (1.78 m) tall and weighs 170 pounds (77 kg). It is known as Hybrid III.

acceleration rate at which speed increases
data information that has been translated into electronic signals that can be moved from one place to another
device something made for a particular purpose or to do a particular job
force a push or a pull

◄ Because of crash-test dummies, car manufacturers have been able to design safety features such as seat belts, headrests, and air bags.

Inside a Crash-Test Dummy

Sensors and accelerometers are placed in different parts of the dummy.

Sensors and accelerometers inside the head measure the force and acceleration that act on the brain.

Sensors and accelerometers inside the chest measure the movement of the rib cage. They take into account the impact of a seat belt, as well as the general force of the crash.

Sensors on the neck measure the way the neck bends and tears when thrown backward and forward.

The arms do not have any instruments, because protecting arms in a car is almost impossible because of the many positions they could be in.

Sensors and accelerometers on the legs measure the twisting, tearing, and rotation of the pelvis, knees, thighs, shins, ankles, and other joints and bones.

The test dummy's **torso** is made from foam, so that the dummy accurately shows how a human torso would be pressed and twisted.

The First Dummies

Before dummies were used, crash tests were carried out using the bodies of dead humans. Some tests were also carried out using live volunteers. The first crash-test dummy was built in the United States in 1949 and named Sierra Sam. Hybrid III, the main dummy used today, was created in 1976.

Word Watch

torso main part of the body

Web Watch ▼

www.howstuffworks.com/crash-test.htm
www.chevroncars.com/learn/cars/crash-test-dummy

15

How Do Hot-Air Balloons Work?

Hot-air balloons work because hot air is lighter than cool air. If a fabric balloon is filled with hot air, the balloon will rise and rise, and it will only come down when the air inside the balloon is cooled.

Parts of a Balloon

There are three main parts of a balloon. The envelope is the light-weight fabric that holds the hot air, the basket is the container that the pilot and passengers stand in, and the burner is the **device** that provides the heat.

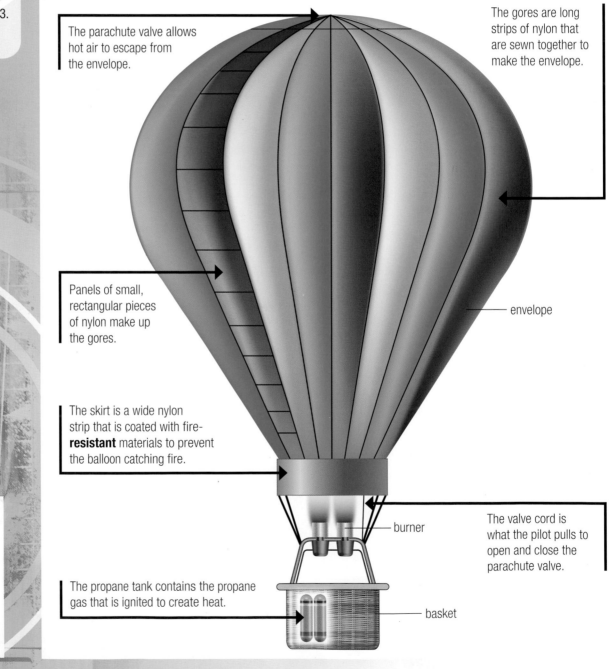

The parachute valve allows hot air to escape from the envelope.

The gores are long strips of nylon that are sewn together to make the envelope.

Panels of small, rectangular pieces of nylon make up the gores.

envelope

The skirt is a wide nylon strip that is coated with fire-**resistant** materials to prevent the balloon catching fire.

The valve cord is what the pilot pulls to open and close the parachute valve.

burner

The propane tank contains the propane gas that is ignited to create heat.

basket

Taking Off

Hot-air balloons are heated using propane gas. The propane gas is released and rises to the burner. The burner ignites the gas, creating a flame, and the flame begins to heat the air inside the envelope.

▲ It takes about 65,297 cubic feet (1,849 cubic meters) of hot air to fill an envelope that will lift 1,000 pounds (454 kg) of weight.

Piloting a Balloon

A pilot makes the balloon rise by filling the envelope with hot air and makes it fall by releasing hot air through the parachute valve. As the hot air escapes, the amount of cool air in the envelope increases and the balloon moves downward. A pilot cannot directly control the **horizontal** direction of the balloon's flight, because the balloon is pushed along by the wind.

Word Watch

horizontal aligned to the horizon
vertical at right angles to the horizon

Back to Earth

For a soft, safe landing, a pilot needs a clear, flat area and a ground crew. Approaching the landing spot, the pilot releases hot air from the envelope. The pilot must know how quickly to release the hot air, without causing the balloon to crash. Ideally, the basket does not land with a thud but skips along the ground a few times. As it does so, the ground crew grabs a rope attached to the top of the envelope and drags the envelope to the ground.

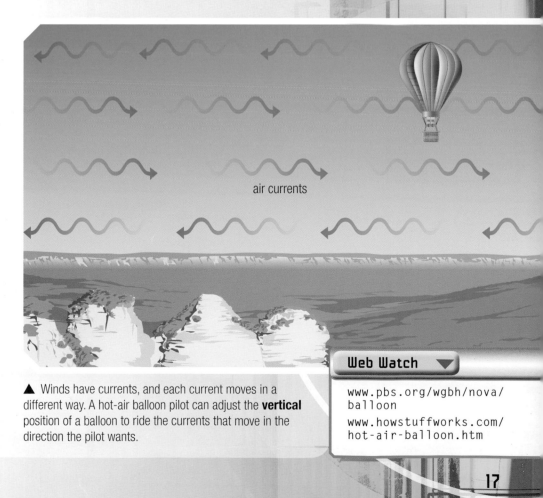

air currents

▲ Winds have currents, and each current moves in a different way. A hot-air balloon pilot can adjust the **vertical** position of a balloon to ride the currents that move in the direction the pilot wants.

Web Watch ▼

www.pbs.org/wgbh/nova/balloon
www.howstuffworks.com/hot-air-balloon.htm

Why Don't the Wings of an Airplane Flap?

Humans have wanted to fly for as long as they have observed birds. A plane does not flap its wings like a bird, but the secret to keeping the plane in the air lies in the shape and use of its wings.

Airplane Wings

Airplane wings are built to copy some of the ways birds' wings work. An airplane's **thrust** comes from its engine, so it does not need to flap its wings. However, a pilot adjusts the wings to change speed and direction and to take off and land.

The wings are the most important part of an airplane. Their shape and the angle of attack create **lift** and minimize **drag**.

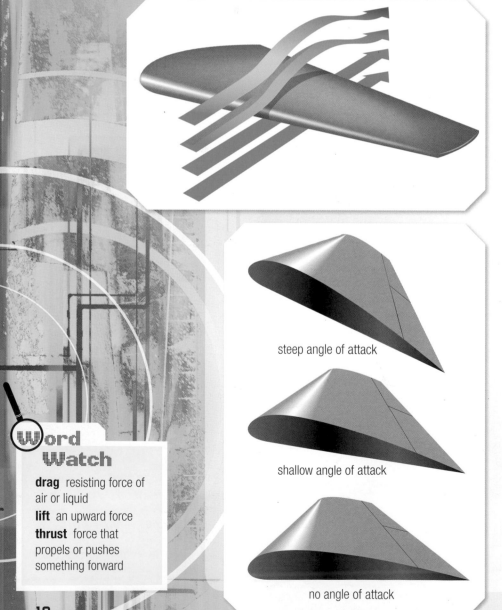

Shape of the Wing

The wing has a shape called an airfoil. The airfoil shape helps the plane lift.

◀ As the airfoil moves through the air, the air flows faster over the curved top than along the flat bottom. Fast-flowing air has less pressure than slow-flowing air, and the greater pressure of the air underneath the wing helps lift the plane.

steep angle of attack

shallow angle of attack

no angle of attack

Angle of Attack

The angle of attack refers to the angle at which the wing is tilted and meets oncoming air. Changing the angle of the wings creates more or less lift. The flaps, slats, spoilers, and ailerons reduce or increase lift and drag, depending on when and how they are used.

◀ A pilot changes the angle of attack depending on whether the plane is taking off, landing, or just flying straight. A steep angle creates more lift but if the angle is too steep, air is not able to pass over the wing and the plane will stall. Less of an angle means less lift.

Parts of an Airplane

Each part of a plane has its own function.

The wing provides the lift that enables the plane to take off.

Air and fuel mix in the engine and are ignited to produce the **force** that **propels** the plane.

Stabilizers control the direction of the airplane.

Ailerons help the airplane roll in the air, and spoilers are raised to interrupt the airflow and create drag.

The rudder controls the position of the tail.

The cabin is the area where the passengers sit.

Flaps can be altered to generate more lift.

The pilot and copilot sit and control the plane from the cockpit.

Wheels are used for takeoff and landing, but are folded into the body when the plane is flying.

Slats can be altered to generate more lift.

The fuselage is the body of the plane.

▲ Most planes have these common parts, from the cockpit to the rudder.

First Flight

The most famous airplane flight in history took place on December 17, 1903, at Kitty Hawk, North Carolina. Orville Wright flew a plane that he and his brother had built. It flew 120 feet (36.6 m). Later that day, Orville's brother Wilbur flew the same plane 853 feet (260 m).

Word Watch

force a push or a pull
propels pushes forward

Web Watch

wright.nasa.gov/overview.htm
science.howstuffworks.com/airplane.htm

How Do Planes Fly on Autopilot?

An autopilot is a **device** that guides particular crafts so they do not need to be controlled by a pilot or driver. Autopilots are not just used on airplanes. They are used to steer boats, ships, and even missiles.

Autopilots and Gyroscopes

Autopilots are designed to work like gyroscopes. A gyroscope is a device that seems to defy **gravity**. It works on a principle known as **angular momentum**.

There are five main parts to a gyroscope: the wheel or rotor, the axle, the inner gimbal, the outer gimbal, and the frame. The wheel is attached to the axle, which in turn is attached to the inner gimbal. The inner gimbal is attached to the outer gimbal, which is attached to the frame.

Inventing the Gyroscope

In 1852, French scientist Jean Bernard Léon Foucault invented the gyroscope. His invention came about as part of his study of how Earth moves.

Word Watch

angular at an angle

device something made for a particular purpose or to do a particular job

forces pushes or pulls

gravity force that pulls objects toward one another

momentum thrust or drive of a moving body

Web Watch ▼

www.gyroscopes.org/uses.asp

wheel or rotor

axle

inner gimbal

frame

▲ The structure of a gyroscope means that its wheel continues spinning in the same direction no matter what direction the supporting frame is tilted at and no matter what external **forces** are applied to it. Toy gyroscopes often use only one gimbal.

How an Autopilot Works

The autopilot was invented by American engineer Lawrence Sperry in 1912. It was basically four gyroscopes, each programmed to detect and correct a different type of movement.

A modern airplane's autopilot is made up of several **CPUs**, each programmed to detect and correct changes in the airplane's course and movement. The pilot has to enter relevant **data** before the autopilot can work.

Pitch, Roll, and Yaw

There are three main types of movements that an autopilot detects. The autopilot then corrects the movement, putting the plane back on course.

▶ Pitch is when a plane moves up or down around a **horizontal axis** from the tip of the plane to its tail. If a plane pitches, the autopilot sends messages to the elevators on the tail of the plane, and the elevators change their position.

▶ Roll is when a plane veers to the left or right around a horizontal axis from one end of the wing to the other. If a plane rolls, the autopilot sends messages to the ailerons on each wing and the ailerons change their position.

▶ Yaw is when a plane twists around a **vertical** axis. If a plane yaws, the autopilot sends messages to the rudder on the tail and the rudder changes its position.

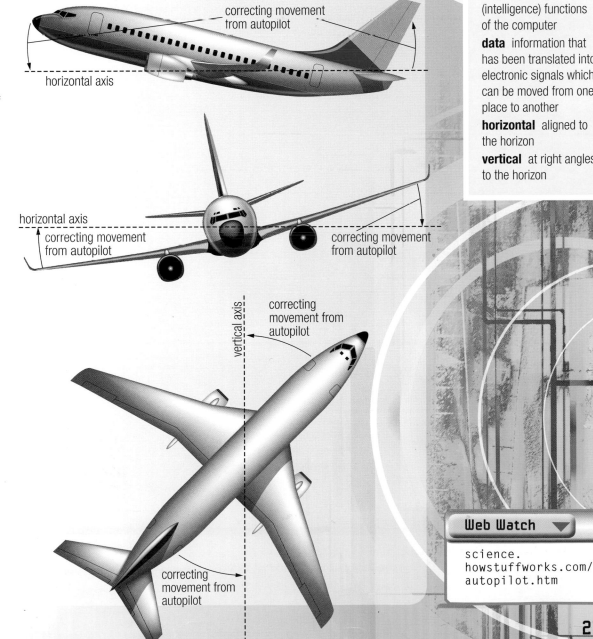

correcting movement from autopilot

horizontal axis

horizontal axis

correcting movement from autopilot

correcting movement from autopilot

vertical axis

correcting movement from autopilot

correcting movement from autopilot

Word Watch

axis imaginary line around which a body turns or rotates

CPUs (central processing units) main units of computers, which contain and control the logic (intelligence) functions of the computer

data information that has been translated into electronic signals which can be moved from one place to another

horizontal aligned to the horizon

vertical at right angles to the horizon

Web Watch ▼

science. howstuffworks.com/ autopilot.htm

Can Spy Planes Fly Without Being Detected?

In 1940, radar technology was introduced and began to be used to detect the position of planes. Spy planes need to fly undetected or "underneath" the radar—as well as avoiding heat and sound tracking systems.

Inventing Radar
Radar was not invented by one person. Research into radio waves in the early part of the 1900s, particularly by the German scientist Christian Hülsmeyer, led the way for the construction and operation of a radar by the British military in 1940.

Radar Technology

For more than 60 years, the ability to detect planes has revolved around the radar. Radar technology works by sending out high-frequency radio waves. If the radio waves hit something in their path, the waves are bounced back to their source and picked up by the radar's antenna. Radar technology measures the time it takes for the radio waves to return to the radar. The distance between the radar and the object can be determined because the speed of the radio waves is known. Radar technology is similar to how an echo works.

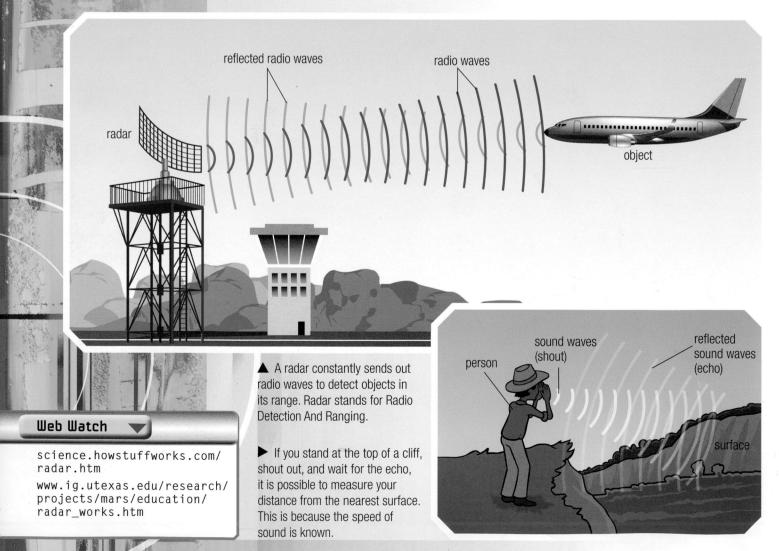

reflected radio waves

radio waves

radar

object

▲ A radar constantly sends out radio waves to detect objects in its range. Radar stands for Radio Detection And Ranging.

person

sound waves (shout)

reflected sound waves (echo)

surface

▶ If you stand at the top of a cliff, shout out, and wait for the echo, it is possible to measure your distance from the nearest surface. This is because the speed of sound is known.

Web Watch ▼

science.howstuffworks.com/
radar.htm
www.ig.utexas.edu/research/
projects/mars/education/
radar_works.htm

Avoiding Detection

Spy planes are generally known as **stealth** planes because they use technology called stealth technology. They avoid detection by radar, as well as by tracking systems that detect sound and heat.

The flat shape of a stealth plane scatters radio waves sent out by radar, rather than bouncing them back to the radar's antenna.

The angles on a stealth plane are shaped so that radio waves are deflected away from the position of the radar.

Stealth planes are coated with special materials that absorb a lot of radio waves.

The engines of most stealth planes are inside the plane, which muffles their sound.

Stealth planes have cooling systems that reduce the amount of heat that can be detected. Heat-producing exhaust is usually released from the top of the plane, away from tracking devices on the ground.

On-board technology reduces the amount of detectable radio energy given out when crews communicate with ground bases and other aircraft.

B-2 Spy Plane

The first **high-tech** stealth bomber was the B-2, which was designed and manufactured by Northrop in the United States. It was one of the first military planes to be almost completely designed on a computer. The first flight of a B-2 took place on July 17, 1989.

Word Watch

high-tech (high technology) advanced

stealth secretive or trying to avoid being noticed

Web Watch

science.howstuffworks.com/stealth-bomber.htm

www.centennialofflight.gov/essay/Evolution_of_Technology/Stealth_tech/Tech18.htm

Why Do Helicopters Fly Straight Up into the Air?

Helicopters can land in many more places than airplanes, because helicopters do not need a long runway. They take off and land **vertically**, using a rotor system. This is not the only advantage helicopters have over airplanes.

A Helicopter's Rotors

The most important parts of a helicopter are its rotors. There is one rotor in the center of the helicopter and one on the tail.

Central Rotor System

The main parts of the central rotor system are the blades, shaft, and swash plates. There are usually two or three blades on top of the rotor system. These blades have an airfoil shape similar to an airplane's wings (see page 18). The blades are connected to the swash plates by the rotor shaft.

There are two swash plates. The lower swash plate is directly controlled by instruments in the cockpit. The helicopter pilot can raise or lower this plate or change its angle. This has the effect of raising, lowering, or tilting the upper swash plate, which controls the angle of the blades.

Tail Rotor

The role of the tail rotor is to **counteract** the **force** from the central rotor blades. If there was no tail rotor, the helicopter would spin around and around as its central rotor blades spin.

Da Vinci's Helicopter

The first known design for a helicopter was drawn by the inventor, artist, scientist, and mathematician Leonardo da Vinci in 1493.

▲ In the 1490s, Leonardo da Vinci drew his idea for an aircraft that looks similar to a helicopter.

Word Watch

counteract work against

force a push or a pull

vertically at right angles to the horizon, or up and down

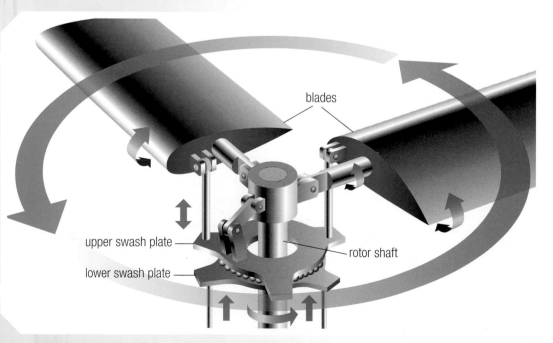

▲ The helicopter's motor turns the central rotor shaft, which turns the blades.

blades

upper swash plate

rotor shaft

lower swash plate

Collective Control

The process involved in moving a helicopter straight up and straight down is known as collective control.

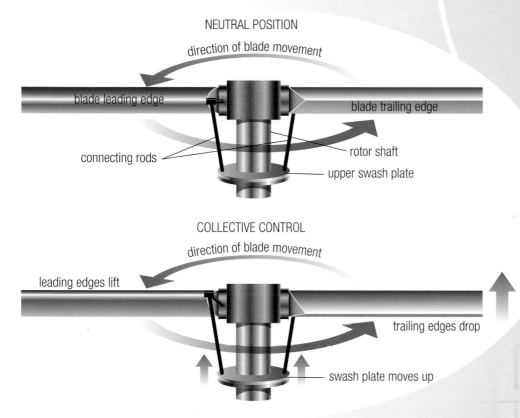

NEUTRAL POSITION

direction of blade movement

blade leading edge

blade trailing edge

connecting rods

rotor shaft

upper swash plate

COLLECTIVE CONTROL

direction of blade movement

leading edges lift

trailing edges drop

swash plate moves up

Cyclic Control

Cyclic control is the process involved in moving the helicopter forward, backward, and side to side.

▼ Cyclic control involves tilting the swash plate so that the pitch of the blades becomes uneven. This causes the helicopter to tip in a particular direction. For example, tilting the swash plate to the right makes the helicopter travel right.

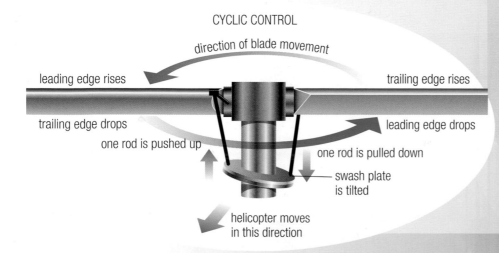

CYCLIC CONTROL

direction of blade movement

leading edge rises

trailing edge rises

trailing edge drops

leading edge drops

one rod is pushed up

one rod is pulled down

swash plate is tilted

helicopter moves in this direction

◄ Collective control involves raising or lowering the swash plate without tilting it. As the swash plate rises or falls, the **pitch** of the blades change but all are the same. This is the right pitch to generate **lift** (see page 18) and the airflow required to lift the helicopter.

(see page 18)

Word Watch

lift an upward force
pitch angle of the helicopter blades

Web Watch ▼

www.centennialofflight. gov/essay/Rotary/early_ helicopters/HE1.htm

science.howstuffworks. com/helicopter.htm

What Was the Space Race?

The space race was a fierce rivalry between the United States and the **Soviet Union** (USSR), which took place from the mid-1950s until the mid-1970s. Both were trying to prove that they were the most technologically advanced nation in the world.

Race to Launch a Satellite

The space race started in 1955 when U.S. President Dwight Eisenhower announced that the United States had the technology to send a **satellite** into space within three years. President of the USSR Nikita Khrushchev immediately announced that it would take his nation only two-and-a-half years to launch a satellite. The race was on!

The United States doubted that the USSR had the technology to launch a satellite. They were shocked when the USSR successfully launched Sputnik 1 into space on October 4, 1957.

Race to Launch Humans into Space

In 1961, the USSR was again first when they blasted **cosmonaut** Yuri Gagarin into a single **orbit** of Earth. U.S. President John F. Kennedy announced that his country would land a human on the Moon "before the decade is out." The United States poured money into its space program. On July 20, 1969, Neil Armstrong stepped foot on the Moon.

ARCTIC OCEAN

NORTH AMERICA

Soviet Union

United States of America

EUROPE

ASIA

AFRICA

SOUTH AMERICA

PACIFIC OCEAN

INDIAN OCEAN

AUSTRALIA

SOUTHERN OCEAN

ANTARCTICA

▲ The United States and the Soviet Union were considered superpowers, because they were the two most powerful nations in the world at the time.

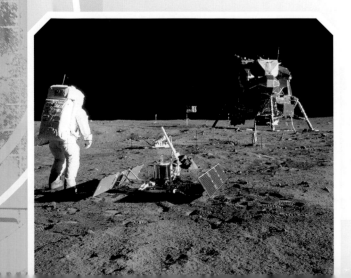

◀ Although Neil Armstrong was the first human to step foot on the Moon, two other astronauts accompanied him on the *Apollo 11* mission, Buzz Aldrin (pictured) and Michael Collins.

The Race Ends

In the early 1970s, both the United States and the USSR established **space stations**. Soon after, the launch of a joint US–USSR space mission in 1975 ended the space race. Both governments had realized that cooperation was better than competition.

Satellites

Satellites receive and send messages to and from Earth. There are several types of satellites, such as:

thrusters

antenna

solar cells

body

receiver

batteries

transmitter

▲ A communications satellite sends and receives telephone, Internet, or television signals.

- communications satellites, for **transmitting** telephone, Internet, television and other messages, **data**, and signals around Earth
- weather satellites, for monitoring weather patterns that help **meteorologists** predict the weather
- military satellites, used by countries to capture images and pick up radio signals from other countries
- navigational satellites, to help ships, planes, and even cars navigate
- scientific satellites, for capturing images and signals from other bodies in space

The main features of a satellite are:

- a body to hold and protect all the equipment
- batteries to power the satellite
- solar cells to recharge the batteries, so that the power never runs out
- motor, fuel, and thrusters to **propel** the satellite into space and keep it in orbit
- antennas to send and receive messages
- radio **receivers** and transmitters to send and receive signals and messages

How Do Rockets Get into Space?

Humans invented ways of traveling on sea, land, and even up in the air, but sending something into space seemed too difficult until the 1950s. They needed a new kind of craft that could reach the high speed necessary to leave Earth's atmosphere, and an engine that did not require oxygen to burn its fuel.

Blasting Off

To understand how rockets get into space, it is important to understand Newton's Third Law of Motion. The scientific law developed by Isaac Newton in 1687 states, "For every action, there is an equal and opposite reaction."

A rocket moves as a reaction to an initial action, such as the ejection of gases behind it. To get out of Earth's atmosphere, a rocket needs to be traveling at a speed of at least 15,500 miles (25,000 km) per hour. To create a reaction that will reach this huge speed, there must first be an action that **propels** the rocket upward.

▶ The bottom section of a rocket contains fuel and boosters that provide the **thrust** to get into space. As the fuel in these boosters is burned, gases rush out the bottom of the rocket, propelling it upward. This follows Newton's Third Law of Motion.

reaction

action

Try This!

Demonstrate Newton's Third Law

1. Blow up a balloon.

2. Hold the end of the balloon, but do not tie a knot in it.

3. Let go of the balloon!

Air rushes out the neck of the balloon, and the balloon moves with the same level of **force** but in the opposite direction as the released air. This is an example of Newton's Third Law of Motion.

Rockets

Fuel needs oxygen to burn, and there is no oxygen in space. Rockets are powered by solid fuel or liquid fuel, which needs to be mixed with an **oxidizer** that can be carried into space with the fuel.

Solid-Fuel Rockets

Solid fuel is used in the boosters that provide the thrust for rockets. This method involves igniting a solid source of fuel that burns until all the fuel runs out. It is simpler, cheaper, and safer than liquid fuel, but it has one large disadvantage: it cannot be controlled. Once it is lit, the fuel burns until it runs out.

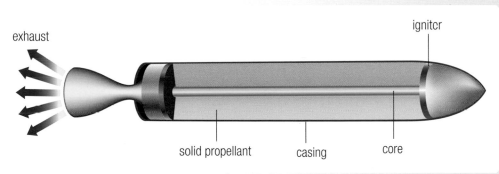

exhaust

igniter

solid propellant   casing   core

▲ When a solid-fuel rocket is ignited, its core heats up and the solid propellant starts to burn. This produces exhaust, which gives the rocket thrust.

Liquid-Fuel Rockets

Liquid-fuel rockets mix liquid fuel with an oxidizer, usually liquid oxygen. This is pumped into a **combustion** chamber where it is burned to create a very high-pressure gas. The gas is forced out the back of the rocket, which propels the rocket forward. This liquid fuel can be controlled in much the same way as the fuel in a car and can be varied to speed up, slow down, or change direction.

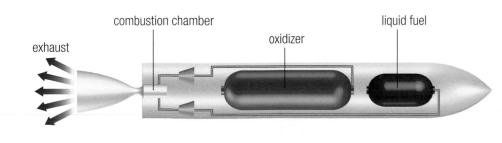

combustion chamber

liquid fuel

oxidizer

exhaust

▲ In a liquid-fuel rocket, the liquid fuel burns in a combustion chamber. The exhaust that is released gives the rocket thrust.

Fireworks

Firework rockets are solid-fuel rockets. They are packed with a solid fuel (mainly gunpowder) and then ignited. The rocket is propelled into the air and does not stop until the fuel source runs out.

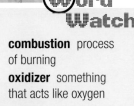

Word Watch

combustion process of burning

oxidizer something that acts like oxygen

Web Watch ▼

www.nasa.gov/worldbook/rocket_worldbook.html

How Do Space Shuttles Work?

During the 1960s and 1970s, rockets sent into space could only be used once. This was very expensive, so the U.S. National Aeronautics and Space Administration (NASA) designed the space shuttle. The space shuttle is a reusable launch vehicle.

Parts of a Shuttle

The three main parts of a space shuttle are the orbiter, the solid rocket boosters, and the external fuel tank.

The solid rocket boosters contain solid fuel. The fuel provides most of the power to blast the shuttle into the air.

The external fuel tank contains liquid fuel and oxygen, which provides the space shuttle with extra power to take off and enter **orbit**. Unlike the solid fuel, the amount of liquid fuel that is used can be increased or decreased by the crew members.

The orbiter is the main craft. It houses the crew of the space shuttle, all the scientific and navigation equipment, and the shuttle's main engines.

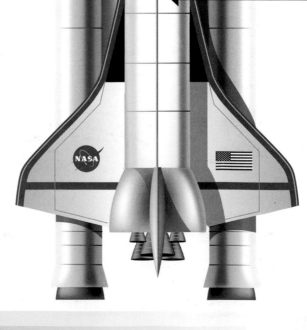

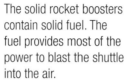

The First Space Shuttle

The first space shuttle was *Columbia*. It took off from the Kennedy Space Center in the United States on April 12, 1981. In 2003, *Columbia* exploded as it reentered Earth's atmosphere, killing seven crew members. It was on its 28th mission.

▲ *Columbia's* first mission lasted for 2 days, 6 hours, 20 minutes, and 53 seconds.

Word Watch

orbit path around an object, such as the sun or Earth

A Space Shuttle's Journey

The design of the space shuttle incorporated technology that could handle the four stages of the journey: launch, orbit, reentry, and landing.

Orbit

Once the shuttle is in orbit, it relies on its orbital maneuvering system (OMS) to keep it on track. The OMS has two engines and two tanks. These tanks contain the liquid fuel and **oxidizer**.

The crew spends most of its time in orbit in the front of the shuttle. This is where the living quarters are, as well as most of the equipment the crew will use.

Reentry

As the shuttle prepares to reenter Earth's atmosphere, it is turned tail first. Then the engines are fired up to slow the shuttle down. Just before it enters the atmosphere, it is turned the right way around, and excess fuel is burned so that the shuttle does not explode on reentry.

Using Space Shuttles

Space shuttles are used to launch satellites and to take astronauts to space to fix old satellites that have technical problems.

Word Watch

deploys moves into position

oxidizer something that acts like oxygen

thrust force that propels or pushes something forward

Launch

The main **thrust** for the launch comes from the solid rocket boosters. The fuel from the boosters lasts for two minutes, then the boosters fall away and float safely to Earth. The shuttle's engines start using the fuel from the external fuel tank. This fuel lasts for seven minutes, then the external fuel tank falls away. It burns up when it reenters Earth's atmosphere.

Landing

The shuttle descends in the same way an airplane prepares to land. It is still flying much faster than a normal airplane, so it makes several sweeping turns to slow it down. When the shuttle is about 2,000 feet (600 m) from the ground, the pilot lifts the nose up and **deploys** the landing gear. A parachute is ejected to help the shuttle stop.

Web Watch ▼

www.nasa.gov/columbia/home/index.html

www.howstuffworks.com/space-shuttle.htm

Index